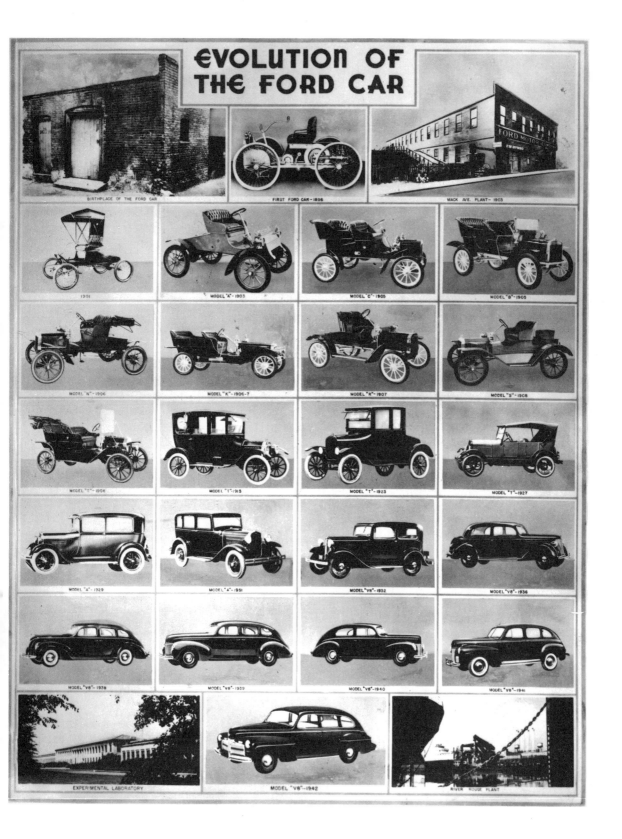

EVOLUTION OF THE FORD CAR

BIRTHPLACE OF THE FORD CAR

FIRST FORD CAR—1896

MACK AVE. PLANT—1903

1901

MODEL "A"—1903

MODEL "C"—1905

MODEL "B"—1905

MODEL "N"—1906

MODEL "K"—1906-7

MODEL "R"—1907

MODEL "S"—1908

MODEL "T"—1908

MODEL "T"—1915

MODEL "T"—1923

MODEL "T"—1927

MODEL "A"—1929

MODEL "A"—1931

MODEL "V8"—1932

MODEL "V8"—1936

MODEL "V8"—1938

MODEL "V8"—1939

MODEL "V8"—1940

MODEL "V8"—1941

EXPERIMENTAL LABORATORY

MODEL "V8"—1942

RIVER ROUGE PLANT

Cornerstones of Freedom

The Story of

HENRY
FORD

AND THE
AUTOMOBILE

By Zachary Kent

CHILDRENS PRESS®
CHICAGO

Norman Rockwell painted this picture of Henry Ford building his first car.

Library of Congress Cataloging-in-Publication Data

Kent, Zachary.

  The story of Henry Ford and the automobile / by
Zachary Kent.
      p.   cm. — (Cornerstones of freedom)
  Summary: Biography of the engineer and industrialist
whose pioneering company showed the world how to build
and mass-produce reliable, inexpensive automobiles.
  ISBN 0-516-04751-5
  1. Ford, Henry, 1863-1947 — Juvenile literature.
2. Industrialists — United States — Biography — Juvenile
literature. 3. Millionaires — United States —
Biography — Juvenile literature. 4. Automobile industry
and trade — United States — History — Juvenile
literature. 5. Ford Motor Company — History —
Juvenile literature. |1. Ford, Henry, 1863-
1947. 2. Industrialists. 3. Automobile industry and
trade — Biography. 4. Ford Motor Company —
History.| I. Title. II. Series.
HD9710.U52F6644 1990
338.7'6292'092 — dc20
|B| 90-2163
|92| CIP
                                                AC

PHOTO CREDITS

Henry Ford Museum — 4, 6 (both photos), 7, 8 (both photos), 9, 10 (both photos), 12 (both photos), 13, 14, 15 (both photos), 17, 22, 23, 24, 27 (right)

Historical Pictures Service, Chicago — 1, 11 (both photos), 16 (both photos), 18 (both photos), 21, 28 (both photos)

Minneapolis Daily News/Historical Pictures Service, Chicago — 27 (left)

Wide World Photos — Cover, 2, 25, 31, 32

Cover — Henry Ford

Page 2 — Henry Ford (right) and his son, Edsel, pose with the first Ford car built in 1896 and with the ten millionth Ford car built in 1924.

His gray eyes blazing with excitement, Henry Ford strode toward the shed door. For months the thirty-two-year-old mechanic had worked in the brick coal shed behind his rented house at 58 Bagley Avenue in Detroit, Michigan. With the help of a few friends, Ford had vowed to build a gasoline-powered motorcar. In their spare evening hours, the men made a simple engine and mounted it on a small wooden frame with four wire-spoked wheels. Ford named it a Quadricycle, although truthfully it looked more like a large baby carriage.

Finally, around 2 A.M. on June 4, 1896, Ford and his friend Jim Bishop tightened the Quadricycle's last bolt. A light rain fell outside, but Ford insisted on testing his motorcar at once. Suddenly, Ford realized that the Quadricycle was too large to fit through the shed's doorway. Without even hesitating, Ford seized an ax. Wood splintered and red dust flew as he chopped down the door frame and knocked down part of the brick wall.

Hearing the noise, Ford's wife, Clara, rushed from the house and watched the two men roll the Quadricycle out into the rainy night. Eagerly, Ford switched on the current from the battery and adjusted the gasoline. "I set the choke and spun the flywheel," he recalled. "As the motor roared and

Henry Ford in the Quadricycle in 1896. The small engine was at the rear of the vehicle (right).

sputtered to life, I climbed aboard and started off. The car bumped along the cobblestones of the alley as Mr. Bishop rode ahead on [a] bicycle to warn any horse-drawn vehicles."

Clutching the long curved tiller, Ford steered his car down Grand River Avenue and onto Washington Boulevard. In front of the Cadillac Hotel, the car coughed to a halt. Curious hotel guests stepped outside and grinned as Ford and Bishop replaced the spring in an igniter. "When we had repaired it," Ford recalled, "we started the car again and drove back home."

Skeptical Detroit neighbors had long called Ford "Crazy Henry" because of his intense desire to build a horseless carriage. In the years following his historic ride, however, many people changed their minds. Ford's hard work and engineering talent would lead him to build improved versions of his motorcar. As a manufacturer, his methods of making and selling automobiles would spark an American social revolution. At the height of his stunning career, half the cars in the United States would bear the name Ford.

Born in Dearborn, Michigan, on July 20, 1863, Henry Ford was the eldest child of William and Mary Ford. William Ford encouraged his young son to help with chores on the family farm but the boy much preferred examining the tools in his father's workshop. Machinery fascinated Henry, and his mother called him a "born mechanic." "When we had mechanical or windup toys given to us at Christmas," recalled his sister, Margaret, "we always said, 'Don't let Henry see them! He just takes them apart!' "

Young
Henry
Ford

Henry Ford's parents, Mary and William Ford

His mother's death in 1877 deeply saddened thirteen-year-old Henry. Two other events that year also changed his life. One day while Henry and his father were riding in their horse-drawn wagon, they saw a chugging steam engine crawling toward them on the road. Portable engines were sometimes hauled from farm to farm for threshing grain or sawing logs, but this one moved under its own power. "I was off the wagon and talking to the engineer," remembered Henry, "before my father . . . knew what I was up to." The thrilling sight of that self-propelled vehicle stuck in his mind for many years.

That same year, William Ford gave his son a watch. Using homemade screwdrivers and tweezers,

Henry kept taking the watch apart and putting it together again until he became an expert watch repairer. "Henry is not much of a farmer, he's a tinkerer," William Ford admitted by the time his son reached sixteen. Grudgingly, Mr. Ford found the boy a job as a machine-shop apprentice eight miles away in Detroit. Henry worked happily among the humming lathes and buzzing drill presses there. Later he switched jobs and worked on ship engines in the boatyards of the Detroit Dry Dock Company. In 1882, nineteen-year-old Henry moved back to Dearborn full of mechanical knowledge. The Westinghouse Company hired the bright young mechanic to demonstrate and repair its steam engines throughout southern Michigan.

Workers at the Detroit Dry Dock Company in 1880

"He was so different from all the other young men I had known," remarked Clara Bryant after meeting Ford in 1885. Following a long courtship, the couple married in Dearborn on April 11, 1888. For three years Ford ran a sawmill on farmland given to him by his father. A new scientific breakthrough had already aroused Henry's imagination, however. In Germany, Nikolaus Otto and Eugene Langen had invented an internal-combustion engine fired by gasoline. In 1891 Ford watched one of these gasoline engines in operation at a Detroit soda-bottling plant. Excitedly he rushed home to Clara. "I've been on the wrong track," he exclaimed. "What I would like to do is make an engine that will run by gasoline and have it do the work of a horse." Determined to succeed, Ford got an engineering job at the Edison

Illuminating Company in Detroit. In a workroom at this electric company, Ford tinkered with designs for gasoline engines during his spare hours.

Ford built his first crude gasoline engine in 1893. After another three years of experiments he at last felt ready to build his first complete automobile. Other inventors had built cars before Ford. Horseless carriages made by German engineers Gottlieb Daimler and Karl Benz chugged along European roads as early as 1886. In Springfield, Massachusetts, a crowd cheered in 1893 when brothers Charles and Frank Duryea demonstrated their motorcar, the first successful automobile built in the United States. But Ford wanted to design an automobile that was better than all the others.

Left: Gottlieb Daimler in his first automobile in 1886, driven by his son. Right: The daughters of Karl Benz in the first Benz car, 1886.

Enlisting the help of enthusiastic fellow workers, Ford spent hours each night in the coal shed behind his house on Bagley Avenue. Carefully they filed cylinder parts and wired an electrical ignition. "Henry is making something, and maybe someday I'll tell you about it," was all Clara Ford would say to curious neighbors.

At last, on that early June morning in 1896, Ford's Quadricycle was ready for its first test. His heart pounding with excitement, Ford made a few adjustments, spun the flywheel, and the engine roared to life. His test drive through the darkened Detroit streets proved his ideas would work.

Scraping money together, Ford designed further improvements such as a stronger metal frame and a more comfortable seat. Clara and their baby son Edsel sometimes joined him as he raced through the

Left: Clara Ford with Edsel.
Right: Detroit, Michigan, in 1895.

streets at astonishing speeds of up to twenty miles per hour. People stared and children chased after the strange vehicle. "Everyone thought Henry was crazier than heck with that darned car of his," recalled George Holmes of Detroit. "They used to say, 'Here comes that crazy Henry Ford.'"

By 1899, however, dozens of small American companies were manufacturing automobiles. Rich people throughout the nation wanted to buy motorcars. In Detroit, lumber merchant William Murphy and several other men decided to invest in Ford. Thirty-six-year-old Henry Ford quit his job at the Edison Illuminating Company to head the new Detroit Automobile Company. One day Ford demonstrated a car for a local reporter. As they roared past the shop of a saddler and harness maker, Ford declared, "His trade is doomed."

The Detroit Automobile Company building in 1900

Inside the Detroit Automobile Company factory

Ford's partners in the Detroit Automobile Company wanted the company to build big, expensive cars. Ford disagreed. He strongly believed that small, cheaper cars would find the largest market and serve the public better. Production slowed to a trickle as Ford spent his time dreaming of the perfect car. Finally his frustrated investors refused to support him and the company failed after one year.

To win fame and fortune, Ford decided to build a racing car. Working around the clock for months, he constructed a two-cylinder, twenty-six-horsepower racing car and entered it in competition against a forty-horsepower car designed by Alexander Winton. On October 10, 1901, 8,000 people packed the Detroit Fairground at Grosse Point to watch the

ten-mile event. Winton held the world speed record and no one thought Ford's car had a chance.

At the crack of the starting gun, Winton's car zoomed off. Ford trailed behind. His race partner, Ed Huff, crouched on the running board, using his weight to keep the car balanced on the curves. Dirt from Winton's tires blew into their faces. Then, after the third lap, Ford began pulling his car tighter on each curve. At last, on the seventh lap, Ford shot ahead and in the end he crossed the finish line first. "The people went wild," exclaimed Clara Ford. "One man threw his hat up and when it came down he stomped on it." Ford took home the $1,000 prize and his victory advertised his name far and wide.

Clara Ford (right) wears a "duster," a long coat used by people riding in open cars on the dusty unpaved roads of the early 1900s.

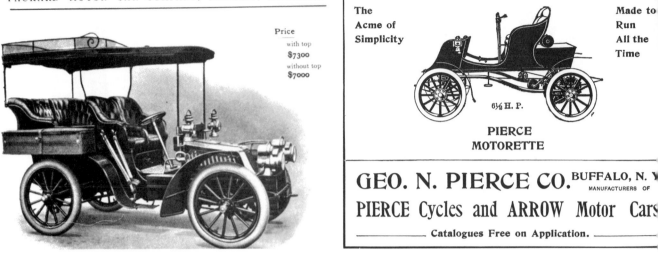

Price
with top
$7300
without top
$7000

The
Acme of
Simplicity

Made to
Run
All the
Time

6½ H. P.

PIERCE
MOTORETTE

GEO. N. PIERCE CO. BUFFALO, N. Y.
MANUFACTURERS OF
PIERCE Cycles and ARROW Motor Cars

——— Catalogues Free on Application. ———

Most early automobiles were expensive. The Packard (left) sold for over $7000 at a time when the average worker made about $600 per year.

Attracted by Ford's growing reputation, a new group of excited Detroit investors promptly set up the Henry Ford Company. "They wanted a car for production," recalled mechanic Oliver Barthel. "[But] Ford insisted on having a racing car..." Seeking the power to do as he pleased, Ford resigned from the company in March 1902.

While American car companies manufactured such popular autos as the Packard, Buick, Pierce, and Oldsmobile, Ford concentrated on building another racing car. Named after a famous express train, the "999" stretched ten feet in length and boasted a seventy-horsepower engine with four massive cylinders. Ford entered the car in a challenge race against Alexander Winton's new car, the Bullet. Ford hired a daredevil cyclist named

Barney Oldfield as the driver. On race day, Oldfield bravely climbed into his seat. "This chariot may kill me," he grimly stated as he pulled on his goggles, "but they will say afterwards that I was going like hell when she took me over the bank." Barreling ahead, his foot jammed down on the accelerator, Oldfield won the five-mile race with a world record time of 5 minutes 28 seconds.

Henry Ford (right) and Barney Oldfield show off the "999" racer in 1901.

Coal merchant Alexander Malcolmson and several other Detroit citizens became the third group to invest in Henry Ford. With $150,000, they organized the Ford Motor Company on June 16, 1903. Detroit machinists John and Horace Dodge, who later became famous car manufacturers themselves, were hired to build 650 engines according to Ford's design. A dozen busy workmen transformed

The Ford factory (above) in 1903. An imaginative 1904 magazine ad (right) called the Ford car one of the seven wonders of the world.

a wagon shop on Mack Avenue into the Ford factory. Here the men assembled engines, chassis, wheels, and other parts into finished cars called the Model A. In July 1903, a Chicago dentist bought the first Ford for $850. "The most reliable machine in the world," boasted company advertising as orders for Fords started flowing in.

In January 1904, to drum up further publicity, Ford climbed onto the seat of the Arrow, another racing car he had built. On a one-mile course across the frozen surface of Lake St. Clair, Ford raced against the clock. "With every fissure the car leaped into the air," he exclaimed. "I never knew how it was coming down . . . . but somehow I stayed topside up and on the course." At the finish, thrilled witnesses rushed across the ice shouting Ford's world-record time of a mile in 36 seconds. As word spread, orders for the Ford Company's new cars—Models B, C, and F—shot up. "Home of the Celebrated Ford Automobile," proclaimed a sign on the company's new Piquette Avenue factory. By 1905, 300 workmen were assembling 25 cars each day. Henry Ford was a success at last.

The demand for cars seemed limitless and Alexander Malcolmson urged Ford to build fancier, more expensive cars for the wealthy. After months of disagreement, Ford finally bought Malcolmson's shares for $175,000 in July 1906 and took firm control of the company. "This is a great day," he said to one of his mechanics. "We're going to expand this company, and you will see that it will grow by leaps and bounds. The proper system, as I have in mind, is to get the car to the people."

Pouring profits back into the company, Ford built a giant new factory at Detroit's Highland Park racetrack. In the meantime he developed a popular new Model N with a price tag of $600. To cut costs, Ford ordered the entire car, including its engine, built under the Highland Park roof. By concentrating on a single standard model, Ford sold a record 8,243 cars in the next twelve months.

"Joe, I've got an idea to design a new car," Ford told his favorite draftsman, Joe Galamb, in the winter of 1906. "Fix a place for yourself on the third floor 'way back, a special room .... and we'll start work ..." Night after night, Ford's team of engineers labored over the new design. "Mr. Ford," recalled Galamb, "...was there practically all the time." "He'd never say, 'I *want* this done,'" remembered another engineer. "He'd say, 'I wonder if we can do this. I wonder.' Well, the men would break their necks to see if they could do it." At last after a year of hard work the team wheeled the first handmade Model T out of the experimental room. "Well, I guess we've got started," beamed Ford.

Following Ford's vision, the men had created the simplest yet most modern automobile ever built. A newly designed magneto system sparked the four-cylinder engine. A never-before-seen planetary transmission made gear shifting much easier. The use of high-tensile vanadium steel kept the Model T sturdy but lightweight. "I will build a motorcar for the multitude," Ford had predicted. "It will be large enough for the family but small enough for the individual to run and care for. It will be constructed of the best materials .... But it will be so low in price that no man making a good salary will be unable to own one ..."

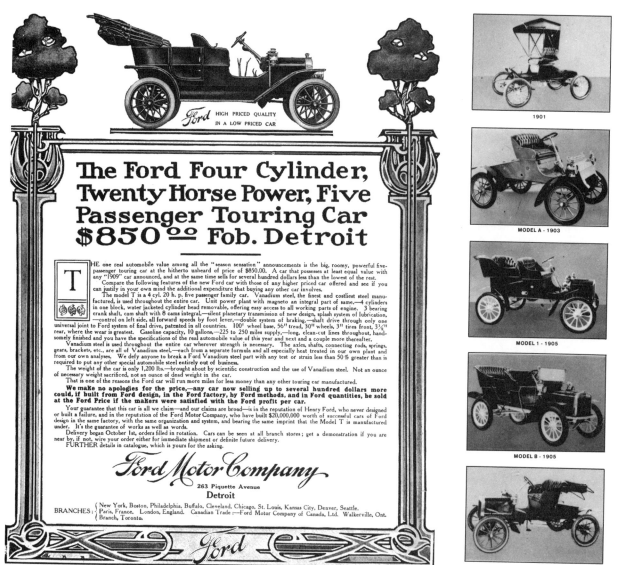

A 1908 magazine ad for the Model T. The pictures at the right show the development of Ford cars from 1901 to 1906.

True to his word, the Model T excited Americans everywhere. Farmers especially liked the car. It bounced easily over rutted country roads with sturdy flexibility. Yet it was strong enough to drag plows or wagons when necessary. Offered for sale at $850, Ford advertising correctly claimed: "No car

This 1903 car featured a tonneau, or rear seating compartment.

under $2,000 offers more..." Happy Model T owners soon nicknamed the car the "Tin Lizzie." Up rocky mountainsides and through deep puddles, it seemed the Tin Lizzie could go anywhere.

To meet the great demand for the Model T, Ford searched for ways to speed up production. He hired more workers and installed the fastest toolmaking machines available. In 1912, 78,440 Model T's rolled out of the Ford factory. During the next year Ford experimented with a new technique to streamline the assembly process. At that time, skilled mechanics worked separately building each engine or transmission from scratch. Walking back and forth from their workbenches they collected nuts, bolts, and other parts from bins as they needed them. To make a magneto, for example, a worker performed twenty-nine different operations.

Now Ford engineers arranged magneto builders along a long table. Each worker performed just one or two tasks before passing the part on to the next person. With this "assembly line" system, workers completed each magneto seven minutes faster. Then Ford installed a conveyor belt to carry the parts along during production, saving even more time. Soon conveyor belts carried other auto parts through the same ingenious process.

Workers building magnetos. Each man performs one or two tasks as the magnetos move down the assembly line.

One day's output is lined up in front of the Ford plant in Highland Park, Michigan, in 1913.

"Every piece of work in the shop moves," declared Ford. "It may move on hooks, on overhead chains . . . it may travel on a moving platform, or it may go by gravity, but the point is that . . . no workman has anything to do with moving or lifting anything." The smooth continuous operation of this first modern industrial assembly line cut the average time it took to complete a Model T from 12½ hours to an astonishing 5 hours and 50 minutes. In the following year, Ford and his enthusiastic factory superintendent Charles Sorensen were able to reduce production time to a stunning 93 minutes per car.

In 1914, the Ford Motor Company manufactured over 250,000 cars, nearly half of all the automobiles

24

sold in America that year. At the same time, Ford kept lowering the price of the Model T to win ever-greater shares of the market. "Every time I reduce the charge for our car by one dollar," he gleefully stated, "I get a thousand new buyers." Year after year, the automobile king cut prices—from $590 to $440 down to $390 by 1914—and still his yearly profits skyrocketed, making him a multimillionaire.

The monotony and pressure of high-speed assembly-line work caused many exhausted Ford workers to quit. Ford soon found a solution to his labor problem. In January 1914, he suddenly doubled the daily minimum wage of his workers from $2.50 to $5. "A magnificent act of generosity," exclaimed the New York *Evening Post.* "GOD BLESS HENRY

Henry Ford (driving) gives Thomas Edison (in rear seat) a ride.

FORD," blared a headline in the Algonac *Courier*. Such high pay was unheard of at that time. "He's crazy, isn't he?" wondered the publisher of *The New York Times*.

The day after Ford's announcement, despite the freezing weather, 10,000 men crowded outside the company gates seeking jobs. Workers lucky enough to be hired proudly wore their identification badges everywhere they went. In time, other factories and industries were forced to raise wages to compete for laborers. With increased wages, America's working class rose into the comfortable middle class, living better than ever before. Henry Ford's ideas had sparked an ever-growing market for his cars.

The assembly line and the $5-a-day wage transformed American industry and American society. Flattered by his sudden, astonishing fame, Ford boldly made an effort to halt World War I, which had been raging in Europe since August 1914. In December 1915, the car manufacturer chartered a ship, the *Oskar II*, in New York City. With a number of diplomats on board, Ford's "Peace Ship" steamed to Norway. Although his peace mission failed, many Americans respected Ford's effort. Democrats in Michigan nominated Ford to run for the U.S. Senate in 1918. Without campaigning for a single day, he came within 5,000 votes of winning

Henry Ford on the *Oskar II*. Reports that the American delegates on board were quarreling inspired cartoons like the one at left.

the election. Recognized as a genius industrialist and a friend of the working man, Ford's fame reached new heights into the 1920s. "We Want Henry" clubs sprang up and people even talked of running him for president.

It was Ford's wonderful Model T that brought him his greatest fame. "Watch the Fords Go By," read a sign outside the Highland Park factory. In the peak year of 1923, the company produced more than 2 million Model T's. Having cornered 57 percent of the U.S. automobile market, the simple black car rattled along roads in every part of the nation and the world.

The solid Model T in basic black (left) met tough competition from the flashier models of other companies in the late 1920s.

In an effort to compete, the General Motors and Chrysler automobile companies enticed buyers with more expensive cars to be paid for in installments. A rainbow selection of colors, powerful six-cylinder engines, and such advances as four-wheel brakes and power-operated windshield wipers attracted growing numbers of buyers to such cars as General Motors' Chevrolet and Chrysler's Plymouth. In the midst of the Roaring Twenties, Americans demanded glamour and change, but the Model T remained the same as ever. People began to laugh at the Tin Lizzies they saw chugging along the roads. "What does the Model T use for shock absorbers?"

asked one popular joke. "The passengers!" Although Ford cut the Model T's price to an unbelievable $240 in 1925, sales fell rapidly.

Finally on May 26, 1927, Henry Ford and his son Edsel walked along the Highland Park conveyor line. They watched as workers welded together the 15-millionth Model T. Climbing behind the wheel of the car, Edsel drove his father out to Dearborn where Ford kept his famous Quadricycle and his first Model T. After a brief ride in each historic car, Ford announced, "Now, we've got to do it." After nineteen years, Ford stopped building the Model T.

Mobs of buyers pushed and shoved into Ford showrooms to see the new Model A unveiled in December 1927. Offered in four colors and seventeen body styles, the Model A immediately claimed a huge portion of America's automobile market.

"My work is all done," sighed sixty-four-year-old Henry Ford upon completion of the Model A. Although he had created the modern industrial age, Ford increasingly seemed to prefer simpler, bygone times. "History is more or less bunk," he said. "I'm going to start up a museum and give people a *true* picture of the development of our country. That's the only history that is worth preserving."

During the 1920s, Ford founded Greenfield Village in Dearborn. Board by board and brick by brick, Ford transported some of America's most historic buildings to the model village. Visitors walked past such homes as those of poet Walt Whitman, songwriter Stephen Foster, and natural scientist Luther Burbank. Tourists visited the Springfield, Illinois, courthouse where Abraham Lincoln once practiced law and the Menlo Park laboratory where Thomas Edison invented the incandescent light bulb. Guides dressed in period costumes showed visitors round village shops, a cider mill, and a farm—all operated just as they were in the 1800s. Today, vacationers still visit Greenfield Village to witness living history the way Ford wanted it remembered.

Sadly, Henry Ford grew increasingly willful and narrow-minded in the 1930s and 1940s. As company president, Edsel Ford did his best to lead Ford Motors forward smoothly. But his father constantly interfered, halting progress, firing loyal company executives, and making life miserable for workers on assembly lines. Henry Ford stubbornly believed he had already built the best cars possible. He refused to consider further change. By 1940, company sales had slumped to just 20 percent of the automobile market. Edsel Ford, his health ruined, died three years later. The hard work and new ideas of Edsel's son, Henry Ford II, would in time help

Henry Ford in the 1903 Model A, pictured with the mode of transportation that his automobiles replaced.

Ford Motors regain its place among the nation's leading car manufacturers.

On April 7, 1947, Henry Ford prepared for bed at Fair Lane, his Dearborn estate. That night, the automobile pioneer died of a stroke at the age of eighty-four. The millions of people worldwide who remembered Ford's great contributions mourned the loss of their folk hero. By making the automobile available to everyone, Ford truly had changed the way people worked and lived.

"It will take a hundred years to tell whether he helped us or hurt us, but he certainly didn't leave us where he found us," declared humorist Will Rogers during the glory days of the Model T. Today, as Americans drive along busy highways, there can be no doubt that Henry Ford's revolution in transportation still touches our daily lives.

Henry Ford at the Golden Jubilee of the auto industry in 1946

INDEX

About the Author

Zachary Kent grew up in Little Falls, New Jersey, and received an English degree from St. Lawrence University. Following college he worked at a New York City literary agency for two years and then launched his writing career. To support himself while writing, he has worked as a taxi driver, a shipping clerk, and a house painter. Mr. Kent has had a lifelong interest in American history. Studying the U.S. presidents was his childhood hobby. His collection of presidential items includes books, pictures, and games, as well as several autographed letters.